CODEPENDENT

The Secret of Our Unconcious Codependency

Michelle J. West

Codependent

Codependent

Copyright © 2021 Michelle J. West

All rights reserved.

Codependent

TABLE OF CONTENTS

Codependent

INTRODUCTION

I t is important to recognize not only the role of manipulated victims but how the manipulation has invaded us, how it modifies our relationships with others and the perception of boundaries between us and them. Behind every one of us there is a very articulated story, which asked us to make choices; some of them taken a long time ago, often without knowing, without wanting, and without an alternative, but which have deeply influenced our identity.

Living as codependents or together with codependents pushes us towards confused feelings of inadequacy, doubt and insecurity.

We, too often realize that others have decided and established for us what is important, and what is right or wrong. Above all, mostly without realizing it, we consider that what concerns the interests and emotions of others is important, but our own emotions, needs, and our simplest pleasures do not seem equally relevant.

Living impregnated in codependency means being specialists in asking others to take charge of our lives and suffer the consequences of having done so. Specialists in surrounding ourselves with people who will constantly know us better than we know ourselves, who will show us what we should do, and the way we should think.

It means anxiety and fear of not being up to it. It means seeing our personal fulfillment only in others and depending on others to accept ourselves. It often means having very intense relationships, in which we feel we have given much more than we have received, thus making us suffer.

Who among us can say we have chosen to feel afraid or inadequate? Who among us can say we have chosen to find ourselves in a condition that we do not like?

One of the most curious extravagances of our psyche is that sometimes we would like to heal but we feel that we will not be able to do it. However, the most difficult part is to accept that sometimes we can heal but we don't want to.

Healing means changing. Changing means losing a part of ourselves and our identity. We could think that losing the so called "sick part" is just a positive thing, but our unconscious psyche does not necessarily share the same opinion. In codependency, changing is a precursor of abandonment, thus healing means facing the fear of being abandoned by others, especially by those who are the mirror in which we see the value of ourselves reflected.

It is a recurrent and proven fact that we should not ignore as during the healing process we might face unconscious but completely real resistances: "Do I have the right to stop to be codependent? What happens to the persons important to me if I no longer take care of them? Will they love me if I do not take care of them? I can be codependent for many other years if I want to, should I resist a bit longer and see if my problems vanish by themselves?"

When we are aware of that, we know that these questions come from unconscious fears, then we accept that none of those questions deserve an answer.

Choosing to heal is worthy enough to heal. Any other person in our environment will have to be able to readjust their relations with us as the independent persons they are or should be.

Once healed we will be more attractive for certain people, and much less for others, and this is how the personal change works.

One of the most immediate effects of healing from codependency is to stop attracting toxic manipulators and to alleviate the pain and suffering from their abuses.

There is another point to discuss about when we want to start a healing process. Healing on one's initiative or on others' request implies very different results. Sometimes, too many people in our environment have already decided to be able to decide what is right for us, and even to decide whether our condition is "healthy or ill."

Our dignity to change arises in our independent choice to heal and to have different relationships.

It is not easy at all to change at the request of others.

Changing at the request of others means not understanding where we should go. They will transmit their vision of change, often with the best intentions, other times as another attempt to manipulate us.

If then, changing means healing from codependency, the requests of others will often sound incomprehensible. Each of them will see only a part of our codependency through the filter of their own maturity, if not through their own selfish needs.

Those who often ask us to heal, they do it with heart and sincerity, driven by the hope of reaching an emotional understanding based on two basic things: the joy of simple relationships and the pleasure of being together but not having the need to "cling" on to one other.

Out of literary context, in our reality, our codependency is not equally intense with everyone.

With some people, codependency is integrated into the relationship without turning into a real problem. With some others codependency attracts toxic and dangerous people. In other cases, it achieves a high intensity only with certain persons and in specific situations, but it becomes very often an out of control issue and mercilessly invades all our relationships.

It's up to us to decide if we should heal from something and if our condition is healthy or toxic, we have the final word as no healing is ever possible if there is no voluntary first step of those who suffer and say "it is enough," "I want more," "I want to feel good with the people I love and whom I respect" and "I am no longer available for toxic relationships."

Most of the time, all this occurs when the suffering and anger that have invaded us outweigh the rest.

If so, you are welcome suffering, thank you for shouting that it is time to change, it is time to choose to change and that it is you, no one else, only you are the one who claims the right to heal. And anger is welcome as well; it's the strongest engine we have to defend ourselves from those who endanger our integrity.

Healing from codependency is the bright feeling of having paid debts with the past and the present; it is the joy of the right to say: now I choose who I want to be and with whom.

Healing is the serenity of looking at the eyes of ourselves and the characters of our life; forgiving to learn from mistakes, asking for compensation if we have been offended; untying ourselves emotionally from those who no longer have a reserved corner as VIP of our lives, and finding the joy to be together with whom VIP has always been and always will be.

So, if you are here reading these lines because your time has come, the biggest gift will be to have the privilege of being by your side and being part of it.

Codependent

CHAPTER 1:
THE CONSCIOUS
CODEPENDENCY

"We can never be quite clear whether we are referring
to the world as it is or to the world as we see it."

Gregory Bateson

When we are codependents, at least we need one "dependent" person to relate with. Without understanding very well why, both characters of a codependent relationship (dependent and codependent) must respect precise rules. One has to live by another one and constantly oriented towards another one. As codependents we "agree" to live for others, to sacrifice our desires, needs, and pleasures in the name of others. The consequence of this sacrifice is to become "caretakers, controllers, or controlled persons"

At the same time, as codependents we accept a condition whereby what others think, feel, decide, will have a direct consequence on our own self-esteem and personal value. Those who play the role of "dependents" must always take care to live in a situation that allows us to help them, acting for them, supporting them, alerting and protecting them, suffering for them or on behalf of them if necessary.

If our dependents are narcissists or manipulators, our codependent nature will be abused by them. The dependents-manipulators drain us of our energies, leaving us unable to pull ourselves out and surrendering to the tormentor sometimes, forever. If dependents are not narcissists or manipulators, the roles of both characters sometimes cross into the others territory, and roles can be exchanged in a way that has always seemed fascinating to me, especially when I was able to experience it by myself.

For example, I may be the codependent mother of a son (dependent), so I will be constantly trying to prolong his dependence on me as long as possible. I will live for him by giving up my own life if my codependency requires that; I will be proud of his success and his success will be mine as well. I will feel worthy or despise myself based on how his behavior and moral are. Then, when the now-adult child grows up distant from me by maturing and living his adult and independent life, this will make me feel abandoned, and I will consider his independency as ungrateful and cruel.

But then, as a codependent mother I will enter the role of an elderly and needy person, that now-adult child will suddenly find himself reactivating the codependent relationship but in opposite roles, that is: as an elderly mother I will have become the dependent one, and he — the now-adult son— will have become the one who takes care of me.

He will reactivate all the dynamics of his childhood but with opposite roles: this time, the son performs as the codependent one, and the elderly mother performs as the dependent one.

So, the roles are the same ones (dependent and codependent) but occupied by the opposite characters.

Within parenting relationships, or in general terms within relationships, there is nothing wrong in taking care of each other. The point is that within codependent relationships, caretaking means sacrifice and the obligation of taking care of somebody as a lifestyle we can't avoid or modulate.

One will feel pushed towards controlling the relationship and will focus attention on the other one's needs and desires. The other will have to live according to desires and needs that are not their own ones.

Because of this codependent covenant between both codependent characters, one lives in the other mixing the boundaries where one ends and the other begins. The dignity of one is in the hands of the other one.

The Signs of a Codependent Relationship

Those who want to understand codependency in-depth, they want to understand how one starts to be codependent.

14

Was it due to a severe childhood trauma? Sometimes it is, but sometimes we are codependent, and we don't feel so tied to a traumatic past.

But then, how is it possible that I became codependent having had a family that everyone would have called normal and functional?

How is it possible that I became codependent and my siblings didn't?

Why was I? My genetics? My fault? Was I unlucky? These and other questions will accompany us together with their answers on this journey that I would really like to experience with you as an immersion from the surface of our conscious codependency, to our dark and unconscious side.

This way will allow you to re-emerge with the awareness to see a 360° image of codependency. Once done, you will be able to see how codependency joined your relationships and how you could get out if you chose to.

Choosing to contact again with those simple relations that we all deserve but in codependency they become complicated and dense. Choosing to modulate the codependent patterns not only with narcissists and manipulators but also with the rest of the people and, not less important, in the relation with yourself.

We will see the childhood trauma, the wound in common with narcissists and finally, we will see how our identity was born and how it can be changed; how we can understand our identity to reinvent ourselves into who we would like most to be.

We will see what love means in codependency, how our idea of love can affect the quality of our lives, and how it can be abused by narcissists and manipulators.

But one step at a time, let's start from the surface, from the most important superficial signals of codependency, those that often unite dependents, codependents, and manipulators.

There are many points in common between codependents and dependents. In my past as a codependent, I often found myself in the position of interspersing my need to give with the need to keep people close to me in order to help me.

In codependency, both parts suffer.

The most important initial step in understanding codependency is to move our gaze from the single trees to look at the wood.

The single trees are the differences between long lists, types and subtypes of codependents and dependents. The wood lets us see the relationship between them, and their points in common.

After all, once out of academic researches, in the real life the main codependent's imperative is not to be alone, the rest has to do with how to achieve it.

We will see how codependency affects relationships much more than the single individuals. It means that the solution passes through changing our relationships with others first. Once done, codependency fades alone. No manipulator can affect us if our relationship with them is or becomes feeble. No abandonment can let us feel bad if we don't experience a detachment as an abandonment.

So, let's start with the signs we have to take into account to understand if codependency is leading our relationships with the important people in our lives.

We will see 13 signs with examples and extra comments. All of them can affect both the life of codependent and dependent. If you are not codependent and you just want to understand better our way to be with others, it will be an interesting reading about our "nature".

If you are reading this with the hope to heal from codependency, it can be somehow scary to find so many alerting behaviors one after the other. No worries: healing from codependency does not mean to eliminate all of them. It means to see what there is behind them and how to manage it.

But it is too soon to talk about healing, this first part of the book is dedicated to what we usually do due to codependency.

We Focus Our Lives on Others

This is the first fundamental characteristic of codependency: constant attention to others, living thinking about others, anticipating their thoughts and judgments, doing everything to adapt our lifestyle based on how other people are made, their passions and experiences. We focus our lives on others much more than on ourselves. It does not appeal to healthy people and generates toxic relations. This behavior can lead to a deep sense of interpenetration with others, not only in couple relationships but in any important relationship.

When we are codependents, we have preferential relationships: we look for people with specific problems or needs for care, and we build a relationship on it.

Since codependents are people oriented to be with others, intuitively we would be led to believe that codependent people must always be sociable and constantly willing to meet new people. It is not necessarily so.

In fact, we are constantly turned towards others, but it is also true that in order to be with others we must identify their areas of need in which we can act to help them; or their areas of strength that we could use as a support to our needs and weaknesses.

Can this be translated into a clear manipulative will? Yes, but the truth is that in most of the cases, codependent people's intentions are not cruelly manipulative. Simply, this is our way of being with others, moving around the needs of others, their desires, and their passions.

Where we identify needs, desires, or weaknesses we will offer ourselves to help; where we encounter areas of strength, we will offer ourselves to make alliances. The intrinsic deal will be the following: I give you my help and my love, and then you give me your closeness to convert it into a stable relationship that gives us security.

When we meet new people and we detect their clear desire for independence and autonomy, or a low propensity to share their emotions, our interest in them will fade very quickly. Indeed, if for any reason we were forced to be closer, not only the chances of creating a good relationship would be low, but very likely, it would trigger a strong critical attitude on both sides. Most people markedly oriented towards their independence and autonomy do not fit with codependents, as well as the people most oriented towards frivolous pleasures.

The fact of being with other people just for fun or extemporaneous pleasures is not particularly attractive for us because we do not see in these elements levers on which to establish long-lasting relationships. No fun lasts forever while a need can last a lifetime.

A very remarkable aspect of this behavior is that the attention of codependents is so much turned towards others that it ends up involving the emotional sphere in a very evident way, besides the transfer of emotions between the dependent and the codependent. Empathy can reach such high levels that imperceptible signals of sadness, anguish, or irritation are immediately captured and amplified by our sensors.

For the rest of the people, it seems impossible to hide emotions.

Sometimes, the amplification is so strong that somebody even tries to avoid contact with our empathy as it could be perceived as invasive.

In a codependent relationship, the distance of the members who require solitude or detachment is experienced with a real pain and frustration.

The codependent person will try to compensate the risk of losing a relationship by increasing efforts to strengthen it.

The more the efforts grow the more the feeling of asphyxiation on the other side is. It has an expensive price, that means: the risk of not basing our relationship on the authentic desire to be together but on the need to do it.

It pushes away healthy people. They feel that we regularly introduce pebbles into the gears of the relationship with them.

We are too anxious about abandonment or we have too intense emotional reactions, a too insistent presence, or the tendency to blame to keep the bond alive at the moments in which it seems to be loosen.

Not less important, it attracts manipulators and narcissists.

They build their relations with us on our need to live for them. Sometimes, they are so well skilled that we do it for the rest of our lives.

We will get back on it at the end of this chapter.

We Seek Happiness Outside of Ourselves

It is difficult for everyone to answer the question "What is happiness?" but, when we are codependent, I think the most common answer is basically "I'm happy if you are happy." A certain point is that for the codependent person it is impossible to feel happy if even just one single important person in our environment is in difficulty.

So, the initial sentence "I am happy if you are happy" it should be translated into the statement "I am happy if all the important people to me are happy at the same time", and it is quite difficult to achieve it even in the most idyllic realities.

Due to codependency, we often seem resigned being undemanding in this sense, most likely because we do not think we are fully capable to be happy, but while not launching into an interpretation of this type, the fact is that codependents do not spend much time and energy on understanding how to achieve happiness. We prefer much more to enjoy the happiness of the people who belong to our sphere of relationships. Their happiness give dignity to ours.

However, there is a moment in which we do enjoy the luxury of unleashing happiness: when we feel that we are falling in love. Falling in love is most likely the time when we feel really happy as codependents. If we think about it, being in love is an ideal situation when we are codependent: we finally feel in the right to concentrate on a person without the risk of being criticized about it.

The same concept of being accused of giving too much love disappears completely as well as the feeling of inadequacy that so often comes to us. If it is true that falling in love is important in everyone's life, it is equally true that falling in love is even more important for codependents. It is lived in a pervasive way and it frankly can give us wonderful sensations as it is the only space only for ourselves. It is our own happiness, and we don't need to justify why we are so happy. We are happy to be ourselves and we feel free. It is a topic that deserves to be discussed, and we will have the opportunity to get back to this later.

Our Partner's Needs Can Be...Too Important

We are willing to find the partner's needs, even if we have to deny our own ones. With this behavior, we get into one of the most critical and ambivalent spheres of codependency. Firstly, if we have a new partner it means that we are talking about a person whom we fall in love recently. As we said before, falling in love is a very beautiful and intense phase for the codependent person, and if normally, we all have the natural propensity to idealize the person we fall in love with, in codependency this tendency is even stronger. Idealizing the person we fall in love with, it means starting a relationship with high expectations but also with an implicit agreement with ourselves: if in general terms, we are prepared to give to others, we will have to give much more to the person we fall in love with, therefore, devoting much more attention to him or her, and being even more empathetic. If we are normally prone to give too much love, in falling in love we suppose that we will be authorized to show all the love we have, and the last thing we would like to deal with it would be to tower any kind of limit to our love.

But according to the most basic principle of human nature, if we give a lot, we expect to receive a lot. If it does not happen, the immediate reaction is a painful frustration.

The first thing we will take for granted will be to be creating a stable relationship with a person who will guarantee us safety and a stable relation. In addition to safety, we will be seeking for gratitude for the love given.

This second point is especially critical. We would expect to be with a person capable to let us reflect in our most dangerous and beautiful part of codependency, that is to say, making ourselves reflect as a person who deserves attention and importance in a directly proportional way to how much love we have been able to give.

When the partner of the codependent person knows how to play, the relationship will sail on calm waters and will have positive connotations. However, when the partner does not respect the rules of the game, the situation could be very complicated.

Firstly, if the relationship does not continue as stable as imagined, the pain of the possible failure will be very intense. As codependents, we live badly the fact of being abandoned but if the abandonment is related to our partner, everything will be amplified. We must not forget that as codependents, we have not only a strong ability to give love but a strong need to do it. So, a situation that it is continuously repeated in the sentimental relationship of codependents is perceiving that our love is not valued adequately.

Sometimes it is sadly true (if for example we are the partner of a narcissist it is always true), but sometimes it is not really like that, ours is a perception distorted by the way codependency we see.

Unfortunately, what humans receive in abundance, and without too much effort, we perceive it as something less precious. And, if we like it or not, this also happens with love. It is a natural and common human reaction.

If we are not codependent and we feel debilitated by unrequited love, we will break the relationship, more or less injured, more or less angry but we will hardly decide to continue investing in a person who, at least according to our perception, has not been able to respond satisfactorily.

On the other hand, in codependency, it is the fear of abandonment, the fear of being alone, the attachment to whom we have already recognized as ours, and it is very difficult for us to let people go. The mechanism that starts is to give even more, and more, and it will never be enough.

If we are talking about a partner with whom we already have a stable relationship, the dynamics of falling in love will no longer be so influential in the couple's relationship. What will instead be always and equally constant, will be the attention paid to the needs of our partner. The dynamic is the same as any other important person in the codependent's life, that is to say: attention to needs, attention to the other person, a strong orientation towards the emotional life of the other, a great need to confirm that we are important as we are a fundamental source of love. The real difference between a common important relationship and the stable sentimental relationship with the partner of a codependent person lies in the quantity. That is to say, the dynamics are the same ones but with the partner, they are more intense. Losing a partner, in the definitive sense with separation like divorce, but also in a more partial form (therefore, feeling that our partner does not seek our support or our closeness) is very difficult to manage for us the codependents. It opens our most painful wound: the wound of abandonment and loneliness.

In order to avoid any kind of departure from stable romantic relations, we are eager to accept very high prices. If then our partner turns out to be a manipulative person, then a person who has started the relationship perfectly aware of our codependent nature, the possible scenarios can be frankly lacerating. A severely manipulative partner will be able to achieve enormous power over our behaviors and emotions, increasing his or her level of needing more and more in everything that concerns attention, pretensions, time and energy, or even economic resources if necessary.

A fundamental aspect of the codependent behavior is predictability. We respect basic and repetitive principles around which we organize our relationships with others. The higher the manipulative talent of the codependent's partner, the higher the knowledge of our behavior patterns and therefore the tactics that must be used to dominate us, at least as long as we still have energy, resources, or possibly money to give our partner.

Our Boundaries Are Not Clear (at all...)

We may have difficulty to perceive the boundaries between ourselves and the others. In the codependent relationship, the concept of boundaries is confused and ambiguous.

When we accept that we are happy about the joy of others, we are sad for the unhappiness of others, and we are worried about the problems of others, we use our energies for others to receive attention, recognition, and security in return.... Well, at that very moment we are accepting that the boundaries between us and the others are not only unclear, but they must not be clear at all. In fact, according to the codependent logic, the boundaries between ourselves and others seem to be counterproductive.

Establishing a clear boundary where we finish and start would undermine almost all the behaviors of codependents.

Setting boundaries means putting an interference in the perception of other people's feelings, their emotions, and, not less important, their intentions.

Losing contact with the important intentions of others prevents us from perceiving beforehand their intention to abandon us.

In the same way, boundaries would prevent us from enjoying all those positive aspects that we saw very well in others, but we cannot see in ourselves. We should say: accepting boundaries would mean accepting to lose all the good things that are in others and we think cannot be in ourselves. The consequences of this choice are easily imaginable: giving up boundaries means above all offering others the ability to enter within us to manipulate us; it means losing the right to feel worthy of existing as autonomous and independent creatures.

Another remarkably thing about the loss of boundaries is that in the codependent relationship we feel responsible about the emotions of others. Somehow it is recognized that the emotions of one leave the body where they have been generated and they migrate to the bodies of others creating a breakdown.

This is visible in the sentences addressed to children:

"If you are not a good boy, you will make your mother cry. If you do not do your homework, you'll see how dad gets angry." (Implicit message: It is not important to do your homework because it is so you will do well in school and you will feel good. You must do your homework to create happiness in one, or not to create sadness or anger in another.)

The examples would be hundreds of them: if you do this someone will be proud, if you do not do it someone will feel ashamed, if you behave like this someone will be worried... In the end, you act in a reality where all the emotions and feelings of one depend on what others do or do not, say or do not say, hear, or do not hear...

In the most dangerous cases, the link between our emotions and those of others can also be created in a truly abusive way, capable of questioning even the dignity of a feeling or a thought.

Questioning the dignity of people's feeling or thought means taking the risk of condemning them to consider themselves unworthy people both in their own eyes and in the eyes of others.

When somebody introduces the concept that others have the right (if not the duty) to judge if your emotions are worthy or not, that person is stating that you must ask someone for permission before feeling happy, or sad, or proud, or excited. Once stated that your happiness could have the sadness of another as a counterpart, you should give up your happiness. Or vice versa: in some way you should ask authorization for feeling sad.

An example:

You feel sad because you would like to start a professional activity that makes you independent. You need to invest on your training to be more skilled and appealing in the labor market. But you do not have the economic resources to do it yet. Then, you try to find support within your network of parents, partner, best friends, family and so on. In a healthy situation, the person who could help you can give you tips and tools to find the money, or those resources that allow you to achieve your goals; he or she could help you providing part of the required money, or simply could listen to you with affection and do nothing more.

In a codependent relationship, the person you ask for support, will be the one who questions your sadness. A simple need, like the will of independency, can activate the dynamic of abandonment in the other one, and the reaction is usually more or less an explicit aggression. A first common reaction is to make you feel guilty for your "extravagant" sadness, or to diminish the validity of your need. It would not be rare to face sentences like: "Training for a professional activity? You have never worked, and you want to start now, why? To go away? Putting our finance in trouble for your crazy ideas? Are you not comfortable now? You have everything you need!

When it happens, your sadness and your will of independency have crossed the boundary of your body and invaded the other one. Once this is done, the other reacts emotionally as he or she feels your emotions as his or her own. Above all, the other person feels to have the right to question you as your change (financial independency is a great change) will affect the relationship with you. Every change in a codependent relationship is a risk to lose contact with the person who is changing. Finally, a "codependent judge" will enter your head and tell you that you have no reason to feel sad, or that your sadness is wrong. If you feel sad, give up your sadness because it is uncomfortable in another person's head.

This is an example of what could happen when we lose our boundaries due to a codependent relationship. We could add many others, but this is especially useful to start to see something hard to accept when we are codependents: within the codependent relationship, both sides can react aggressively if the other person wants to leave, and both sides can be manipulative or can try to avoid separations. As codependents, we can be the ones who frustrate other's desires to be independent, or we can be the ones frustrated if we need some kind of independency. It means that as codependents we can be victims (if we live with a narcissist, we are clearly the victim), but we can also be abusers, if the dependent person could leave.

When we relate to narcissists manipulators, we can be only the victim. When we relate to any other person, the abuse can flow in both directions as a way to preserve an important relationship.

That's why talking about "codependent people" is not really correct, we should talk about "codependent relationships".

Codependency is intrinsic in relations not in individuals. The lack of boundaries reduces the distance with others much closer.

Who defends this vision usually says: "If codependency is somehow inside of you and not in the space between you and others, why don't you try to be codependent on a desert island...?"

This statement opens a huge debate not suitable for this book but it's still a fundamental note to face the problem of codependency much better.

Once accepting that, it's easier to accept that healing from codependency does not mean to modify our essence but to change our relationship style, and in the next chapters we will see how to do it.

Our Control Creates Toxic Relationships

We control ourselves and others without giving importance to the negative consequences of difficult or deeply toxic relationships. When we are codependent, this represents the group of behaviors more than any others, can damage our psychological and physiological safety. This is the group of behaviors in which the so-called "wound in common with the narcissist" is revealed. Just as narcissists are very capable of controlling and manipulating codependents, in the same way, codependents try to control those people with whom they have important relationships.

Normally, the manipulative capacity of the codependent never reaches the extremes of the narcissist, partly because we do not have the will, and partly because we are not capable.

We maintain a deep capacity for empathy for which we cannot go beyond a certain level of control because we note the suffering under the controlled person.

It is significant to see that while intense control is considered as an indispensable skill for the narcissist, for the codependent person control is experienced as a necessity only when the relationship could be out of reach.

However, in the case of codependent manipulation, the suffering that can result from it often becomes the main reason to get out of codependency. That is to say: either our suffering caused by abusive and cruel manipulators, or the annoyance that we generate in the healthy people we love is the real detonator that let us get out of codependency. Our suffering pushes us to wonder: "what do I have to do to cut away that anguish from my important relations?" "How can I get rid of this feeling of confusion that prevents me from rejoicing, loving, and be loved serenely?"

When that suffering is permanent, the fact is to be able to convert it into a personal choice to change. Changing for ourselves and not for others. This is a Key Point we will often face in this book.

We Can Be Proficient Caretakers

We are specialists in taking care of people, and we identify the unhappiness of others as an attribute to be resolved. In the most extreme cases, this type of behavior results in the conduct brilliantly named as the "Savior Complex" — That is, the unsolicited help of someone who insists on giving it to you.

According to the official definition, a person with the "Savior Complex" feels the unstoppable and constant compulsion to "save" or "rescue" others.

They are, somehow, people in search of individuals in need of help, people ready to help even at the cost of sacrificing not only their own needs, desires, and aspirations but even ready to put their safety at risk.

These features lead to some of the most harmful and toxic relationships that may exist whether they are couple relationships or more generally, family relationships, relationships between friends and even work colleagues.

We face the summum when the person to be saved is a hidden cruel manipulator. This is the most dangerous relation possible for a codependent and the most difficult to be broken.

The codependent gets into the relationship to rescue the manipulator from sadness or anguish and does not realize to be the only one to be rescued from manipulation and abuse.

In codependent couples ruled by the "Savior Complex", therefore, none of the members can feel edified and happy, or at least not for a long time.

The ones who depend the most on love will lose their self-esteem gradually, while the others will feel increasingly burdened by the difficult relationship.

In the codependent couple created by those who have this type of complex, the role of "rescued" and "victim" is mixed in a confused way.

The relationship can be so suffocating that the "rescued" ones cease to understand if they feel inept because they are, or because as rescued people they have implicitly lost the right to take care of themselves. Or rather, they feel that they will never be able to live again except as persons to be saved for the rest of their years. For this reason, they pass from feeling cared for to feeling that they became the victims of their saviors.

The frankly curious part of this behavior/complex of codependency is that, despite being dysfunctional, it can be rewarded socially.

It can even lead us to become famous and influential people in the world of the so-called "institutional caretakers"; for example those who stand out for daring actions aimed at defending human rights in extremely dangerous locations, helping people in difficulty, or aimed at solving expensive environmental issues especially concerning the protection of animals.

If we look carefully at the "Savior Complex", we can understand the key to the codependent relationship: the intensity can severely change but codependent relationships are based on the need to be together much more than on the will or pleasure of being together.

Our Unhappiness Is…Different

We tend to connect our unhappiness with the guilt (of others…). When we are codependent, unhappiness takes on a completely different role if we are feeling it in others or ourselves.

In others, it is translated into an element that attracts us. We know that we can manage it, understand it, and that it would be a noble reason to be together and take care of those who suffer from it.

While, if we perceive this same unhappiness within us, the result is completely different.

If it is natural and necessary for us to take care of others, we experience as an unforgivable distraction the fact of taking care of ourselves.

Dedicating time and energy to ourselves distracts us from what is happening in others, it distracts us from what we perceive as our main mission in life: living for others and through others.

However, recognizing unhappiness in ourselves forces us to turn our attention to ourselves and we do not like that at all, but it goes beyond our will; it's a physiological reaction that we cannot avoid.

When we feel unhappy, our whole-body folds in on itself, leaving out others to dedicate itself to its unhappiness.

This, however, is a luxury that we cannot afford as codependents. The luxury of paying too much attention to ourselves sounds like the risk of losing sight of others. For this reason, our first reaction to our sadness is to diminish it.

If my sadness is not so important it will be less important to deal with it, and even less to resolve it.

Unfortunately (or fortunately), sometimes the unhappiness that we perceive within us cries so loudly that we cannot ignore it. And here, when the volume of our unhappiness is too high, our mind starts mocking and boycotts us.

Our mind distracts us from our unhappiness by turning our attention to the faults of who generated it. "I am unhappy because of you, of your fault, for the malice of one, or the slander of another."

Said in this way it does not seem negative, indeed it seems healthy attention towards the origin of something that made us feel bad, so understanding it should help us to feel better.

In the reality of the codependent person, it does not work exactly like this, the narrative that is created is much more similar to: "Look what you did to me, I am unhappy because of you, for what you said, for what you did, for what you don't have done..." So the focus of attention shifts from our unhappiness to the actions of others, therefore it moves away from us to focus on the wrong activities of others which, sometimes wrongly, sometimes rightly, will always find themselves responsible for our emotional state.

Understanding this is essential to understand a codependent who wants to stop being codependent.

Taking for example the mother-daughter relationship. Imagine that in this relationship the favorite daughter decides to move to another city, therefore moving away and limiting the possibility of spending time together.

This is a typical situation that seriously undermines the mood of a codependent mother.

It is a situation in which her unhappiness cannot be silenced, and which will result in blaming her daughter's decision to leave as an ungrateful and cruel choice.

From the moment this dynamic is activated, the possibility that the reaction of the codependent mother is linked to internal motivations that do not allow her to manage the detachment with serenity is eliminated. Once activated this narrative, the only thing to decide will be whether or not her daughter will have the right to move, if she

Codependent

decided that autonomously, or if somebody else convinced her (clearly in a case will be more guilty than in the another one). Whatever the result is, whether the daughter leaves or not, it will be very difficult that the next step does not sink into guilt.

The guilt will result in a sentimental noose that will follow the daughter regardless of the choice she will take: If she renounces to leave, she will do so in the name of the guilt that has been infused in her, so the noose will tie her to the hardest knot.

If instead, she moves to any other city, the noose will follow her as a sense of guilt and will be the main point of connection with the codependent mother. For her part, the mother will have solved two problems according to the unconscious laws of codependency.

First problem: although in the case of not being able to sabotage the departure of her daughter, she will have maintained a bond with her distant daughter through guilt.

Second problem: She will have somehow removed her unhappiness by focusing her attention on the "guilty behavior" of her daughter. Regardless to the distressing situation created, codependency has been saved, attention to others has been preserved, the bond with the daughter seems to be under control.

From the codependent perspective, the mission can be considered accomplished as this seems the best result possible.

We Are Empathetic People and Difficulties Attract Us

Difficulty and complexity constantly accompany codependent relationships. The difficulty comes mainly from intimate relationships:

35

couples, family members, colleagues, or simple friendship relationships. Outside these contexts, complexity will be related with problematic social environments.

For example, voluntary works aimed at intervening in very complex social realities. Being immersed in certain realities means that those realities also follow us at home. When it happens (it happens quite often) this ends up breaking into the codependent's family too. Those who experienced it firsthand will have examples of single-family homes that suddenly look like reception centers.

All in all, this type of complexity is not necessarily dysfunctional, it can indeed contribute very positively in the social contribution, not only of the codependent people but of their family too. Some of them often receive recognition and commendation for the activities carried out in the social sphere and it can be considered a noble activity.

The complexity that interferes the most with the quality and well-being of codependent relationships is the one that interferes with parenting and relationships of couples. It is as if a dense hood managed to wrap our main relationships, converting them into an explosive mixture that is difficult to handle. Serene relationships and the joy of simplicity seem to be an expensive extra reserved for others.

This is often because empathy leads us to immediately identify the emotionally complex situations of the people we know. The strong need to intervene will then do the rest. But the most relevant aspect of all is the bundle of stratagems that the codependent person puts in place to be with others, not to lose contact and to ensure that he or she is not left alone. We do not have to forget that the relationship with the codependent must always be lived between at least two people in which each one plays a more active or passive role, the controller and the controlled, stronger or weaker, etc. So, the complexity ends up multiplying by two, as each one of the two main characters in codependency is reflected in the complexity of each another.

We Experience Anxiety and Depression

We often accompany our propensity towards others with symptoms of anxiety and depression. This is most likely the easiest behavior to understand from a clinical point of view. It is the aspect most directly related to our physiology and to understand it, it is necessary to understand the physiological meaning of anxiety and depression. Starting from anxiety: if something causes us fear, the immediate consequence is to feel just fear. If this something is a recurrent danger that could frighten us at any moment and in various situations, the biochemistry of fear changes, and produces anxiety.

If then our recurring fear —later anxiety—, has to do with the loss, then our physiology leads us to depression.

In codependency, loss, abandonment, and detachment are the recurring fears of the codependent. Among other things, being so empathetic and oriented towards others, makes us feel their fears as if they were their own ones.

It's now easy to understand why codependency is often accompanied by anxiety and depression. We could say that behind the great success of self-help books against anxiety and anguish there is, also, a large group of codependent readers.

We Need to Delegate Our Decisions

In codependency, it is difficult to make decisions independently. This behavior also invades numerous daily decisions that seem to be impossible enigma without having advice and reassurance from people we consider important.

This is a "constant variable" of codependency and very often our explicit request for advice is suggesting an implicit request to push other persons to decide for us. We can be really and sincerely grateful if their final decision satisfies us. Having support in our decisions makes us feel accompanied and lets us consolidate the bond with the person who helped us decide, and, in this case, codependency looks like a pleasant and positive element for us.

A first little problem arises, however, when the decision made for us was a bad decision. What to do when this happens? Whose fault was it? What should happen next time? Should we ask more advice from that persons, should we ask them to make decisions for us that should be ours anyway? Or should we ask those who have made the wrong decision to be more skilled the next time?

A second bigger problem arises when who made that decision for us is the manipulator of our life and therefore, the last person in the world we should call to make decisions for us.

This is one of the many typical situations of codependency in which any answer to the questions just asked will be wrong. Any reaction of the codependent to a situation like this just described will be wrong.

This is because the situation arises on a logical fallacy, which neglects the main problem: to focus on alternatives that are proposed as the only possible ones without being so. In other words, the main problem is that the person who had to make the decision did not make it. But suddenly the main problem will be hidden behind the false one: if whoever took the decision, without having to do it, was or was not up to it.

Self-Esteem and Self-Love mean "Avoiding Conflict"

We give importance to the esteem and love of others, less importance to self-esteem and self-love. We repress the conflict for fear of losing the support or approval of other people. It might seem we are linking two separates topics, but the connection between the two statements will be more evident very soon. Healthily living the conflict implies two main points:

- In many conflicts, one part should win, and the other part should lose.

As the self-esteem of others seems more important than ours, we don't really like winning in a conflict as it possibly will damage the self-esteem of another person so, in consequence the quality of our relationship. We should say we prefer losing but... who can prefer that?

- If the conflict is not resolved, the relationship may break forever.

Within codependency, those two assumptions are too difficult to manage as the greatest risk is precisely to put risks into the relationship.

In the codependent's mindset, breaking relationships means opening doors to the fear of being alone and abandoned.

In codependent relationships, therefore, the conflict must be managed in a more complex way, it must be more indirect and subtle. Explicit anger must appear as little as possible so that the conflict slips towards guilt and sadness. However, considering that it is impossible not to get angry, anger sooner or later appears quite explosively if not exactly in a dramatic and theatrical way.

This is the typical anger management mentioned in the personality tests "passive aggressive" profile, that is to say, a locked up and suppressed anger which, event after event, frustration after frustration, grows more and more until it explodes, often in the most unexpected moments, thus leaving all observers quite surprised.

When we observe attacks of aggressive passive anger in another person, our first reaction is not to understand how an element that seems so minimal and negligible may have generated such a furious anger.

In fact, we are not considering that small element as nothing more than the last straw that made the vessel of the codependent overflow, or to put it better, it blew the vessel up.

This anger management takes on a very precise role in the relationship between codependent and narcissist: The victims of narcissists accumulate offenses, humiliations, frustrations, and sooner or later, let themselves go to an attack of fury. Then, narcissists will throw it back just with the same violence.

They classify very well as insignificant what detones the victims' anger and manipulate them. They will plunge the victims into the doubt of being exaggerated in their reactions and unfair with the manipulative abuser.

Passive aggression is probably one of the most convoluted and fascinating aspects of human relationships. First of all, because when it becomes a normal personality trait it hides an infinity of complex psychological events behind it, but also because it offers multiple nuances capable of inspiring real thrillers and horror stories; the smile of the aggressive passive is one of the typical elements that make us short-circuit the reading of verbal and non-verbal communication, or rather the reading of facial expressions suddenly seems to be disconnected from what our body is perceiving.

The fact of seeing a smile on a face should make us feel relaxed and calm, while the smile of an aggressive passive can instill a deep sense of confusion if not of restlessness.

That smile shows a "yes" that is actually a "no", or should mean an

"I agree, I will do it" with a silent phrase that says "I don't even know how you could ask me such a thing"

In the worst case, the smile of the aggressive passive is simply the dark precursor of what a person is thinking of inflicting on others shortly thereafter.

Within toxic relationships, passive-aggression can affect both the victim and the abuser. It becomes a dysfunctional way to manage conflicts and repressed violence.

Regrettably, the only way to solve this dysfunctional reaction is breaking the relationship. It might sound easy, but it doesn't as we all know.

We Delay or Postpone Projects and Actions

When we are codependents, starting projects or doing things without someone's help is difficult. This pushes us to delay decisions or to avoid initiatives.

It could be often one of the biggest limitations when we decide to quit a job.

Leaving aside the fact that it is very difficult for us to work as an entrepreneur since it would imply centering ourselves almost exclusively on our own needs as a businessman/woman, even the fact of moving to a new job seems an existential dilemma.

Firstly, the dynamic of leaving a job in the codependent's mind sounds like the dynamic of breaking relationships with important people, as we said one of the biggest difficulties in codependency.

Secondly, the low self-esteem that we have as codependents pushes us to believe that having won a selection process once must not lead us to win it even a second time, and if we succeed it will certainly be a worse workplace than we have today.

This also makes it difficult to achieve independency or to be independent of a partner if our role within relationship involves not working.

If looking for a job is considered as a difficult mission to accomplish, looking for a first job could turns into a real impossible mission, especially if when doing so we would visualize ourselves as people who do it alone, sometimes in secret, and facing the risk of being rejected.

Too many fears to be managed simultaneously, we normally prefer to postpone.

We establish symbiotic relationships

…And not only that, but we can experience the change of the others as precursors to abandonment. This behavior can happen with every important person in the codependent's network but it's especially blinding in parenting and couples. In parenting, codependent parents know that their children will soon leave to form another family.

The temptation to find more or less unconscious stratagems to delay this moment as long as possible can be openly dysfunctional, sometimes trespassing in behaviors that analyzed through the lens of codependency seem only a genuine and profound parental attack, but can provoke deep family conflicts and lacerating sensations of guilt or inadequacy on one side, and abandonment on the other one. Siblings' partners never seem good enough, any decision about their professional and personal independency seems to be the right one, and every autonomous and personal decision about the future will be questioned or criticized.

Sometimes, the best decision seems to give up: when it occurs, we see that somebody never looks for a partner or never finds a job.

When it moves through the decision to start a familiar therapy, normally it highlights how the codependent parents overprotected their children, increasing their dependency and avoiding autonomous decisions, and how it started to open the crisis long time before.

Even if it is less usual today, another fairly widespread behavior until a few decades ago was to choose among the siblings "the sacrificial victim" whose destiny would be to remain forever at home with his or her parents with the mission (never fully recognized) to take care of them.

In many cases, this decision was implicitly and silently accepted not only by both parents and the chosen daughter or son, but also by the brothers and sisters of the victim.

It's amazing to see how this practice can be started by narcissistic or codependent parents with the same probability. The only main difference between them is that the narcissistic parents choose to act fully aware about the meaning of their strategy. On the contrary, the codependent parents achieve the same result but because of the fear to be abandoned.

This tacit pact has more concrete chances of success by preventing the chosen son or daughter from finding a stable couple to live with. When this happens the planned strategy of the family triangle is foiled by the presence of a consort who somehow had to find a place to join the family.

This tacit agreement between parents and victim, however, must guarantee the fairest possible compensation. For example, the chosen son or daughter would have to receive an economical life support while living in the parents' house, thus obviating the economic effort of buying a house or the need to find a full-time job.

Outside parenting, in toxic/romantic relationships this behavior causes a deep dependency on the partner. It will be especially lacerating if we are codependents and our partner is deeply manipulator. The narcissistic partners, for example, change so much once our sentimental relationship becomes stable, and our fear to be abandoned will be used against us. When it happens (and it happens very often), immediately, we accuse them of not loving us as they used to do in the past and to be looking for the right moment to leave. Our first irrational strategy to save the relation is to control the partner and to do any effort to deserve love. For us, it is not easy at all to accept that our narcissists never changed, they are just showing their original and real nature. This generates a recurrent dynamic: we accuse them basing on the right principles (You are not the person I thought, and you don't love me), but our perspective is wrong (narcissists are showing who they really are and our perception of love was based on a mirage, on a manipulation). Above all, that change is not a precursor of abandonment, it's the beginning of a stable betrayal. It generates a strong crisis in the codependent partner. Self-esteem and self-confidence disappear, our identity seems to be suddenly changed and we do not understand who we are. Month after month, year after year, we lose clarity and our energy. Gradually we depend on a toxic relation that we are calling love.

We Have an Obsessive Fear of Losing Our Partners

This is one of the best-known aspects of codependency especially when the sentimental relationship with narcissists comes into play. As codependents, we establish harmful relationships with narcissistic/manipulative partners, and we need to replace (urgently) a finished relationship with another one. The greatest thing that can happen to codependents is to have many important relationships, or within their families, or friendship and professional relationships.

When this happens, we can count on the support of many other people, and the urgency of replacing important relationships that have ended is not so strong. In the same way, we won't need to keep sentimental relationships, albeit painful or unsuccessful, due to the impossibility of imagining ourselves alone. When it happens, we are able to understand that we are maintaining a relationship not safe for us, but somehow, we are unable to pull ourselves out except after long suffering, abuse, and humiliations.

When we have a narcissistic partner or in general, a partner capable of manipulating us, our need to live with him or her it is translated into a strong tool of coercion: when in fact we are tired of abuses, humiliations, and harassment, and we show clear signs of wanting to separate, we are promptly accused of wanting to leave not so much because the relationship doesn't hold up, but because we "like leaving to be with an another one". This accusation is not casual at all; manipulators know very well that we have the impulse to find another partner as soon as possible, so they use this manipulation in part to check if we already have another person in mind, in part to act on our guilt and to modify our self-perception using the true weakness we have against us. The result is basically that they seem the abandoned victims and we are completely wrong; often, we trust them, and we have to find the way to amend our "crazy ideas".

Behind this behavior, there is again our deep attention towards others and a feeling of bonding beyond the sincere affection that, who really love us, often fail to understand.

But this last sentence hides many meanings. The most important is the one too hard to accept when we are codependents: those who most respect our codependency are the ones who do not keep a lasting relationship with us.

I speak about those people who at first appreciate our ability to love and dedicate ourselves to them, but then they move away once they realize that our behavior is born with the need to do it, or the impossibility of not doing it.

These people vanish and we experience them as ungrateful, often just as cruel people when they are just the ones who respect our dignity the most.

They simply come out of our relationship of friendship, kinship, or couple because they realize that we are fueling a behavior, or painful emotions in the name of codependency, not in the name of safe love or self-love.

This is one of the main sources of the famous phrase "codependents love too much," a phrase so frequently used when trying to explain the typical tensions of codependent relationships.

It is an uncomfortable situation for healthy people but also a very suitable opportunity for manipulators.

That's why we are so open to have harmful relations and partners, sometimes in a very repetitive way. And that's also why the narcissistic-codependent combination seems the only union possible for codependents.

Let's try to be as assertive as possible here: it is not! We can be perfectly able to have nice and healthy relationships. Sometimes, we perfectly know that, and we just do it. Sometimes, we need to have more clarity about how to do it.

The union between a narcissist and a codependent can be the equivalent of the human formula of nitroglycerin: explosive and unstable.

Narcissists live for themselves, they give as little as possible, and require as much as possible. Codependents live for others and give as much as possible in exchange for the most stable and reassuring relationship possible. It seems the perfect couple, but it is the scenario of sentimental tragedies, where manipulation and old wounds bring the two sides together in one of the most dysfunctional imaginably couples.

The narcissistic-codependent couples are so frequent and prolific on psychological problems (especially for the codependent who will face constant abuse) that some books on codependency seem to be related to narcissism.

Those who want to recover from codependency cannot ignore the risk and consequences of contact with narcissists. But the narcissistic-codependent relationship is so complex and multifaceted that it deserves a special book ("Narcissists" is fully dedicated to that).

It is necessary to understand in depth the attraction between codependent and narcissist, but it is crucial to move away from the temptation to limit codependency to the relationship with narcissists or psychopaths.

Narcissists and codependents attract each other but healing from codependency and healing from narcissistic relationships are two separate topics.

For us, the narcissistic abuse is so painful and so emotionally scary that sometimes, our all life we focus on the effort to live far away from them. When it happens, narcissists become the center of our existence, even if they are physically away from us.

But, if we could make the narcissism disappear just pushing a button, our codependency would be still there, looking at ourselves and wondering… "So, now what? Who is your next dependent? Who is your next toxic relationship or your next symbiosis with?"

Once we are ready to look beyond them, we are ready to look at ourselves and our self-image changes. It means we are ready to heal from codependency.

With that been said, now it's time. It's time to talk about them: narcissists and how we land in their dark area.

It is our first diving in ourselves and it will not be the only one we will do together in this book.

Codependent

CHAPTER 2:
THE UNCONSCIOUS CODEPENDENCY LOVE AND SELF-LOVE

"In the child, consciousness rises out of the depths of unconscious psychic life, at first like separate islands, which gradually unite to form a 'continent,' a continuous landmass of consciousness. Progressive mental development means, in effect, extension of consciousness."

Carl G. Jung

The first part of this chapter is entirely dedicated to the incredibly strong attraction between narcissists and codependents and it is fully based on one only proven psychological effect: Childhood trauma. Later, we will see that it's not the only approach possible but it's a mandatory step to disclose hidden pieces of codependency.

It allows us to see with clarity how past experiences can get into our unconscious Self and determine our future, but also how the kind of love we give and receive can activate long-lasting changes in ourselves.

The approach of childhood trauma properly explains how narcissistic parenting can generate both codependency and narcissism in children. Above all, it is a useful tool to see why narcissists and codependents are so complementary, tied by a joint wound: the traumatic fear of not having enough love to survive.

The Joint Wound of Codependents and Narcissists

Narcissistic parents treat their children as objects and usually manage them as an extension of themselves, or exactly like "things," using them as narcissistic supply, to nourish their ego.

These parents use the child's natural ambitions to manipulate them towards their narcissistic purposes, as if the child were a part of themselves, an extension they use to improve themselves as egoist adults, thus feeling superior. These parents will pay attention to their children and will most likely satisfy many of their needs, but only on the condition that they must satisfy the needs of their parents; just as healthy people would treat an object: if we need an object, we treat it properly to make it last longer and to make it work better.

If certain objects are especially prestigious and can give meaning to life, such as a beautiful home, a luxury car, or a commercial property, then in the same way narcissistic parents treat their children as something to look at, and to show off. They give the impression of love through their propensity to highlight them in public, to praise them or to appear publicly destroyed by their failures.

On the contrary, another extreme is when manipulative parents see their children as uncomfortable and annoying objects in which case there is nothing the children can do to satisfy or nurture the narcissistic nature of their parents. These children perceive that whatever they do or feel will be discarded or smashed. They can do absolutely nothing to obtain sincere attention or real respect for their emotional needs. The only important needs will be those of the narcissistic parent; these children are simply seen as an inconvenience, a nuisance, or something to be endured.

If it is true that these two extremes of the relationship with narcissistic parents exist, then, it is also true that there are all the intermediate gradations and a child can be treated a bit in one way and a bit in the other one. In some cases, things are done in unison by both parents, however, this differentiation is already marking two destinies: those children will be narcissists, or codependents.

Those children who cannot get any attention, are the ones who are unable to feel appreciated because they are continuously "demolished", devalued and not recognized, then they develop the idea that there is not love for them.

These children begin to think and believe that the world is nothing more than a hostile place, devoid of any form of affection or kindness. These children then act in self-defense, closing themselves off from others, they do not develop a connection with others, do not develop empathy and are convinced that the only way to get love is to steal it or to take it by force because kindness is not beneficial.

These children create an alter ego, an imaginary visionary of the world, where they are sovereigns, and people are objects to be exploited and manipulated. When it happens, gradually but quite quickly, these children become adult-narcissists.

What they have learned will be used to manipulate or destroy their victims; people will be the objects they have been as children. As adolescents or adults, it will be impossible to make them happy, it will be impossible to satisfy them but their victims will have to try to do it, in order to confirm their superiority, their correctness, or their social status.

They will compulsively delegate their prestige to important people in their life, people who will have to recognize them, desire them, envy them… exactly like they had to do with others when they were children.

They will feel entitled to take what they want from others, to do what they want with others, and to do what they want to others.

On the other hand, those children who were treated with love linked to their usefulness as objects, that is those who have been loved under a basic condition: I give you my love if you serve me, if you make me happy, if you take care of me, if you take care of my present and future needs, if everything you do will make me a happy and great parent…

Well, those children have a different destiny in front of them — codependency.

These children develop the idea that people can only love them if they need them, or rather to say, they can love them in relation to how useful they can be to them.

These children will be especially permeable to the needs of others, to the will of others, and to the emotions of others. They will need to be especially empathetic; they will listen and observe a lot.

These children have accepted they must live in function of others, but also that others may not be explicit in the needs they want to convey to them. They then carry on paying close attention to all the verbal and non-verbal messages of the important people in their lives.

These children have "accepted" that their importance does not exist per se but is directly proportional to what they can do for others and how they can help others.

Their worth must be transferred to others, so their goal is no longer to defend, preserve, and increase their own value, but to defend, preserve, and increase the value of important people to them.

Two durable personalities have been created: the personality of the narcissists, almost impossible to heal especially because they hardly recognize that they are narcissist. But also, the personality of the codependents, who sooner or later will suffer so much forcing them to want to change.

This is why codependents and narcissists often come from the same environment, from the same conditions and therefore, from the same wound.

Narcissists chose to dominate, exploit, and give up empathy while codependents chose to serve and to give up their pleasures in the name of the pleasures of others.

In one case the importance of others as persons is denied, in the other case the importance of oneself as a person is denied.

This explains why when we talk about codependents we must talk about narcissists: because unfortunately, due to this wound in the past, they still vibrate together with the sound of the same melody.

As mentioned above, this creates one of the first short circuits of the narcissistic-codependent relationship.

On one hand, codependents offer to give a lot and not ask for an exchange, on the other hand, they suffer from the fact that they have nothing in return.

Narcissists will use this situation by creating a strong state of confusion based on the implicit affirmation: *"You give me what you give me only because you want it, how dare you ask me something in return?"*

This dark commitment throws a handful of salt on the original codependent's wound, namely the fact of being forced to give love with the false hope and conviction of not needing to receive it back.

Narcissists have no interest in letting their connection with the codependent die. Not even in cases where the relationship is experienced as tense and painful for both parts.

They have no interest because their mission is to suck energy from people. So, the only reason that can push them to let a codependent person go is when the codependent stops being one.

For their part, codependents will do everything possible to keep the relationship up and will blame themselves for the failure if they fail.

The life and well-being of the others are more important than their own life, and anyone who tries to shatter this image of them will receive misunderstanding or even attacks from the codependent.

This is because codependents, just like narcissists, are judged by the fact of being codependent or narcissist and both will feel attacked in the deepest part of their essence and story.

Both the narcissist and the codependent harm others and themselves. Narcissists do not know they are hurting themselves, they know that are hurting others, and do not see it as a problem.

Codependents do not understand they can hurt others, they know that are hurting themselves, and although are not completely aware of their condition, they feel remorse and great confusion for this.

But this allows them to open the door of healing. Their suffering let them ask for help, suggestions, psychological support, recovery, and personal growth.

Healing from codependency is not easy because it means going against the deepest part of our identity, but it is possible. We can stop attracting narcissists to our lives forever and it allows us to get closer to healthy beautiful people who did not want to be with us so far, simply because they didn't want to manipulate us.

Let's go ahead in our diving. In the next chapter, there are not narcissists or past in common with them. There is space only for us and for our "dear" codependency.

If you are ready to see the most intimate part of our unconscious, you are ready for the deepest dive we will face here.

The Dark Triple Pact in the Unconscious of Us the Codependents

Here we get into the heart of the book, and also into the heart of codependency, the point where we cross the door of our unconscious past, the point of no return where our journey towards healing from codependency begins.

The point where it all began, when we "decided" even against ourselves, to be codependent. It all started with a triple and completely unconscious pact with ourselves, and we will now recall it.

- First pact

I have no reason to exist for myself as I have no value on my own. My value is the one of those who agree to stay by my side in exchange for my dedication to them, thus sharing with me their value, their dignity, and their esteem.

- Second Pact

I must be constantly present and fundamental in the lives of the people who are important to me, thus ensuring a prominent place in their lives. Otherwise, I would not be in the proper position to check up on them and take care of them, and the proper consequence will be to be abandoned.

- Third Pact

The only thing that matters is having the people I need alongside me: their affection, their acceptance, and the warm feeling of belonging give reason to my life. Therefore, I will repay all this with the most precious possession I have: my love, all that I can and must give, without any reservations if required.

Within that unconscious triple pact, our love was converted into "too much love".

That was the moment when we gave up on ourselves, the moment when we decided that taking care of others could not be just a pleasure but a necessary obligation for our survival.

From that moment on, our pleasure of giving ourselves to others has become something beyond our control.

It is important to listen to the worlds of our triple codependent pact: understanding them is all we need to understand codependency.

This distant and unconscious pact must flow freely in our consciousness, as something that emerges from the secret of our past without any fear of being judged.

It is part of us, indeed, one of the most important parts of us.

Seeing that unconscious pact today does not mean accepting it as a part of us in the future, it means embracing it and starting to understand that it has made its time as today we no longer feel loyalty towards it.

When our triple pact merged with the deepest parts of ourselves, we pretended to forget it.

We can still pretend to deny it, but it is what you, me, and every other codependent have in common.

Some details could change but the bulk of our lives had been decided by those unconscious words; we had become codependent and had accepted a long and implicit set of guidelines. But none of them needs to be valid still in our emotional life if we don't want to.

The Guidelines of the Triple Pact

The latent ghost of our pact is still there, and we know it. Even in happy moments, we hear the echo of that fateful moment when we "accepted" to feel wrong, inadequate or incompetent; this consideration makes us insecure and leads us to have a low evaluation of our value and our abilities.

Because of those unconscious words, our relationships arise from the essential need to stay with people who give us the feeling of never being alone.

For us, the very concept of "being alone" is synonymous of deep anxiety, often real anguish.

If we are codependent, we live with the idea of being incapable of autonomously facing the events of life. Undertaking the effort of independence can create a strong contradiction: autonomy and independence should be positive goals for us, but a secret part of our mind translates both words into another one, "solitude".

Because of those unconscious words, without the presence of a person at our side, we feel easily lost, empty, and useless. For this reason, we require explicit reassurances and confirmations from others, we tend to live any gesture of estrangement, even if minimal, as a possible and painful abandonment.

The absence of a meaningful and caring relationship makes us perceive the emptiness, the feeling of absence of purpose, in the most extreme cases this makes us feel like annihilated persons and without any consistency.

In order to avoid the dreaded abandonment, we work to ensure the constant presence of the others, many times investing unimaginable energies for people who ignore the nature of our triple secret pact. As codependents we must be particularly skilled in understanding the will and needs of the others. We pretend to make them feel good by anticipating their desires. Because of that, simple phrases said by another person to report an implied mood or need, will be automatically translated into an explicit request for us.

I do not know how many times I have experienced it in my life; statements like «It's cold» become, "Bring me a blanket" or "Stand up and switch on the heater".

«I'm bored» sounds like "Do something for my entertainment".

Based on this unconscious reaction «I want to have sex» can easily mean "Please me!"

The Fate of Our Unfulfilled Expectations

Every pact creates expectations and it does not change for unconscious pacts. The point is that a conscious pact can be usually executed, an unconscious pact normally can't. Why? Because the unconscious does not respect the logic of conscious. We must have conscious and logic references to understand the bases of our relationships.

That's why it's so difficult to tell a dream. Dreams are based on illogic patterns, even if we remember a dream well, it's difficult to speak about it, we never find the right words and if we want to go ahead, we need to lie in some details, or we have to invent something.

When we are codependents, something similar happens. If we want to speak about our codependent relationships, we must lie to ourselves but still the logic of our unconscious pact dos not match the illogic consequences of what we must do to respect it.

Let's put ourselves in the best possible solution for a codependent: we stand by the side of who we want, husband, heartfelt friends, brothers, or sisters, let's feel free to choose the best relationships we have most in mind now. There are not narcissists in our lives, we do not have any risk of abandonment on the radar, and no sociopath at sight.

Well, even in this wonderful position, who can be so perfect as to coincide completely with us? Who could even manage to give us what we are unable to give to ourselves? Respect, safe love, recognition, acceptance, esteem and self-esteem, joy, emotional serenity...

Having a codependent personality, even in the most extreme cases, can never reduce us to docile automatons guided by the always right will of others. Eager to comply with the will of the others, without personal goals and perspectives? Come on...

Our desires still exist, they are often mortified and put in the background, possibly we cannot distinguish them and satisfy them, but they cannot disappear into thin air.

In other cases, however, we feel that our autonomous desires are clearly there in our mind. Sometimes, they are ambitious projects, sometimes, they are just small things of daily life: we are conscious of having different purposes from our partner for example, or simply different tastes, even for very common daily activities: we prefer one movie to another, to meet or not certain people, going out rather than staying at home, saving a bit rather than emptying a credit card...

But if we do not feel supported by the approval of our partners or any other referential figures (e.g. parents, colleagues, friends...) how difficult is it to manage these daily lives?

When the other's expectations are not compatible with ours, we suddenly feel the approach of the inexorable sense of obligation. It whispers to us to conform, to be satisfied, and it is very difficult to silence it.

Does it give us the confidence to satisfy our codependent obligations? Yes, but nobody likes the obligation feeling, we can accept it, but we don't like it, even if we are codependent.

The result? Frustration, an "inexplicable" emotional rebellion, feelings of constriction, and anger towards those who forced us to accept things that we would not have wanted to accept.

As said above, anger and disappointment are extremely critical for a codependent: they can lead to the feeling that the relationship is wavering.

This idea sooner or later would be unsustainable, it triggers the alert abandonment precursors.

The triple pact calls us to order, we decide to preserve closeness, trying to ignore the origin of our bad feelings. We assimilate then, we support and accept what we have to do… and once again we have to lie to ourselves in order to respect the logic of our illogic unconscious.

Seen like this, there mustn't be a way out but, in fact, there is, and soon, you will start to see it too.

Our Past and Our Present

Why should it be useful for us to bring to light what we all had been able to relegate to our forgotten past?

The power to cure our past acting on our present can be wonderfully strong if we want to. But time does not exist in our unconscious. Our unconscious does not understand the passage of the years, it does not understand the concept of time at all. Our unconscious does not forget, does not forgive, it preserves the intensity of its unconscious reality and never changes it. Our unconscious pacts are hidden but are fully able to act in our present.

In order to be relegated to the past, a pact must be conscious, it must enter our temporal sphere to be truly and definitively part of our past and as such, stop influencing our present.

We just did this. Once a pact becomes conscious, we decide if it still deserves our loyalty or not.

It's a huge step, it can change us forever, without any haste, leaving us time to contemplate it, to understand its scope, its depth and the meaning it has had for ourselves. If we are to dwell on its true meaning and on its true value, we will see loyalty, the loyalty we have always guaranteed to it, regardless of the cost that it had for us. Even in the most difficult situations to sustain, even in the most painful situations we have respected, protected, and hidden our unconscious pact from others and ourselves.

Now, the time has come to understand that it was a pact only with ourselves and with no one else. Our loyalty to the triple pact is loyalty to ourselves. Only we can break the pact because we have created and accepted it. No one else has, just us.

Deciding to break the pact will have the only consequence of taking away its value because we no longer need it today. Breaking the pact with ourselves just has to do with permitting us to change, and to establish who we want to be.

Breaking the pact is marking the distance with our past to reinvent our present. That is to say: "I want to live fully in my present and to build my future from my present. I want to respect pacts with my conscious will, be the person I want to be, surrounded by the nice relationships I want to have."

This is the wonderful power of our firm declarations and is much stronger than an unconscious decision taken so long ago that we do not even remember we have done it.

I chose to break the pact and the pact is broken; it ceases to have power over me.

Nothing else is needed, we don't need to know how to do it, we don't need solemnity. We just do it. Breaking the pact with ourselves is the first thing we do before feeling that a nice new present can be possible, real and… We deserve it.

How Our Unconscious Pact Affects Our Idea of Love

Breaking an ancient pact is easy if we want to, but the point is "How do I replace it now? Where do I start again?" From love, and without a shadow of doubt.

Codependency is identified by giving too much love. How many times have you heard that you have given too much love?

Love is the atomic nucleus of our feelings, it involves very large spheres of our being, of our emotions, and above all, it involves our relationships with others. For several things, we the codependents, cannot feel up to par, but in relation to love, we are not second to anyone. Where to start from, if not from our major resources?

As codependents we are great love specialists; love is our great engine, our strength, and our connection with the world.

They even accuse us of having too much to give. What does it mean? We are talking about love, after all, how can love hurt us?

Well, that old pact was thus far the breaking point. The need, the obligation, the fact of feeling forced to give love, the fact of not being able to stop, even when we realized that we were throwing it away to the wrong people. Almost nobody understands the meaning of our love well because nobody knows the real existence of our ancient pact: sometimes, it had the power to convert "I love you" into "I need to love you."

Manipulators, oh yes, they understood very well what to do with our love. For them, it is never too much. Just as they understood the power of our ancient pact better than we did, and for this reason we felt so attracted to them, after all, no one else is more able to understand us, in fact they understood us much more than we were ever able to understand ourselves.

Nonetheless, if I think about my story of healing from codependency, I remember hearing about too much love was not enough. Being told that I was giving too much love, all in all, I liked it, it was the recognition of something that I felt was mine and the fact that it was too much didn't seem negative in itself.

If our love is our instrument to build new and nice relationships it is important to clarify how it can be experienced as too much.

It is easy for us the codependents to recognize if we love too much, even in cases where we cannot stop loving and we see ourselves reflected in the misunderstanding of those who ask "Why are you doing this? Why don't you leave him? Why do you stay with her? " Or even, "Why don't you leave me alone?"

But there is another more difficult part to manage and admit: in order to maintain our own identity as codependents, we are forced to resort to abuse, guilt, and moral blackmail as well as narcissists and manipulators.

This implies two consequences: we give love and it does not get back properly: healthy people move away from us and we find ourselves pronouncing words that provoke suffering in both sides: *"Look at all things I've done for you and you're not grateful"* or *"Look how much I sacrificed myself for you and then, why? You don't give the value of it!" "Look how much money I have spent on you and you consider it mundane and normal."*

How is it possible that something is so special and important to us and is not equally valued by the important people in our lives?

When we think about our toxic relationships with narcissists, or psychopaths, it is easy to understand our role as victims: we put ourselves in the position of being exploited and they do it without any mercy.

On the other hand, when we think about our problems in relationships with healthy people who sincerely love us, everything seems more confusing and foggy in our thoughts. Why?

What are we relying on to judge whether behavior in response to our love is right or wrong?

Especially if we are not talking about manipulators who have used and deceived us but simply people who, from their so-called normalcy, have made us feel bad too often, betrayed, deceived, and once again debased and under-valued.

Did we behave better when we found ourselves in similar situations?

Yes, most likely we did. We have satisfied and made so many people happy with our love, since we were children, when without realizing we entered the world of codependency head-on.

A grandmother who told us "You're such a good child, come to visit me every day" (If you don't come every day you won't be seen as so).

"I love you because you are always so kind to me, and help me not like others who only think of themselves" —so don't think about yourself, think about me and so I will love you. — "What a good boy you are, you brought me this and you did this... you always defend me."

Sometimes, a codependent has an explicit violent background but not always.

In most cases, the abuse was more delicate, subtle, often unaware, almost imperceptible to the conscience but clear to our unconscious.

It is also for this reason that, when we want to get rid of a condition of codependency it is not so easy for us to recognize that our problem comes from the people who took care of us.

When we can recognize the wickedness of adult people or simply those who were elder than us as girls or boys, it's painful but less complex for us to untie ourselves from that type of memory, emotion, or relationship with them.

Paradoxically, it is more difficult when we cannot distinguish well the healthy love that we have received from the unhealthy one, above all, because our love for them is still alive even if surrounded by a veil of confusion.

These doubts and questions lead us to the second most important point of our journey towards change, the crucial need to fully understand what love is for us, this love we talk about so much. When many people talk about such an important thing, it is urgent to understand if we are all talking about the same thing ... or not.

Love, Choice, and Shared Pleasure

Love is the most important thing in our life, and it is perhaps one of the most difficult elements to define and understand.

If we look carefully, what is the meaning of giving love, what idea do we have about love? What is the meaning of giving too much? If giving love is an objectively beautiful and noble gesture in which way should it be a problem to be solved?

If the problem of the codependent is to give too much love, where the indicator should be fixed, the bar that tells you that up to here the love you are giving is right and healthy, and from here onwards unjust and sick?

If these answers are difficult in themselves for anyone, they are even more difficult for a codependent person who has the main strength and beauty in love.

Here no one will ask you to stop, in fact, thanks for all the love you are capable of giving, if love is at the center of your attention, it cannot be considered something to give up.

The point is that, if this thing called codependency flows into our love, with how much we give, how much we receive, how much it should be right or wrong to give and receive… well, at least it's very important to agree on what we mean by love.

What is your idea of love?

Perhaps no one will ever be able to give the perfect definition of love, because even love is not perfect. Yes, I would like to share the definition that I gave to love when I decided to get out of codependency.

If it will serve you as much as it has served me, it would mean that you are about to take the second big decision towards your recovery from codependency.

"Love is the choice to make available our cleanest and most beautiful energies for ourselves and others with the only purpose of achieving shared pleasure."

Accepting this as love makes codependency and manipulators disappear from our lives.

Occasionally, it takes some time to let the words enter our soul. It takes time when they come from a loved one and it is needed more time if they come out of a book.

So, let the words do what they can do and focus on the doubts that this form of loving sometimes provokes.

A common doubt when somebody listens to that definition of love is: should the love we dedicate to a sick or sad person not be considered love since it does not give us pleasure?

What shared pleasure can it give to us to be with people who suffer, in difficulty and sad but needy?

Does this mean that love only addresses frivolities, pleasures, and being together only in good times?

Absolutely not.

But let's get into the merits of these moments, let ourselves be carried away by doubts and see if this love should stop being valid at the sad moments of our lives. If we use our most beautiful and cleanest energies to stay alongside a person who is suffering and having the pleasure to keep us close, this person is receiving pleasure from our attentions and from our love. If we have chosen to be there, we will also be feeling the pleasure of making our love available at a moment of suffering that involves both the person we help and ourselves as involved in the relationship.

The beauty of love shines with the same intensity in both positive and negative moments of life.

Love stops shining if we lose touch with sharing pleasure and with our choice to stay there. Our explicit choice to make our most beautiful energies available to people, and therefore the most precious we can give: love. Love stops shining if we leave ourselves out of the love we choose to give to others.

Not only if we neglect to include ourselves, leaving us completely out, but it stops shining even if we leave out some parts of us, the ones we don't like, those parts we leave in the darkness to not see them.

When we choose to love only for the shared pleasure it means choosing to love ourselves, first of all, in our totality not only the part that we like. Choosing to love ourselves is a binary code: either we choose to love ourselves or we don't choose to love ourselves.

A Spanish doctor who later became a famous lecturer, usually says in his lectures: "We cannot love ourselves partially. It is like being pregnant, I have never heard anyone say I am partially pregnant, or you are pregnant, or you are not."

I feel like adding a sentence to it: when we are pregnant and we realize that we are about to become mothers… it is like a "click" inside us, it makes us understand that we are mothers and we will be mothers forever, that's the moment when we start being mothers.

When we choose to love ourselves, the same thing happens: we feel that we have started to love ourselves forever. That's the moment when our life changes forever, when we stop being codependents.

As mothers, we could learn to be always better mothers, as people we can learn to love ourselves, but we cannot learn to love more parts of us.

This is a choice that warmly embraces us in all our parts, recognizing the same dignity to each one. It is the choice that connects us to our greatness. For the rest of our lives.

So, based on that, does love have to be conditioned or unconditional?

When we choose to love like this, there is another difficult question from which we the codependents cannot escape once we decided to change our way to love: should love be conditioned or unconditional?

It depends on who is our love for. Based on this idea of love, healthy love between adults must be selfless but conditioned.

Conditioned on what? At a price. And the only allowed price for love is love.

Nothing is more uplifting, noble and enriching than giving love in order to receive love.

It's quite different to give love to receive attention or dignity. When we are codependents, sometimes, we give love to feel accepted, in order not to feel invisible, ignored, useless, or insignificant.

If love were a coin, it would mean emptying and exhausting our love resources, or deluding ourselves with the idea that we can repay love with a coin that, in fact, love is not. Selfless love is giving love just in order to receive love.

It is not so important that the currency of exchange is the closeness of another person, belonging to a family, the right to feel recognized and accepted. Acceptance, recognition, the sympathy of others, protection and even the beautiful words that we can receive from others in exchange for our love is not love.

They are important, they are beautiful coins, but they are another currency.

If we pretend to give love to those who do not give us back love, we will be overconfident. We would ask love to be what in fact it is not, has never been, and will never be: a coin able to regenerate itself without receiving love.

Unconditional Love

What does remains about love given just for nothing? The conditional love that accompanies the relationship between adults puts us in a position to bring together those resources that allow us to take care of very special people.

At least for many years, they are not able to return what they have obtained, as they are not able to return our love consciously: these people are our children, the only people worthy of receiving an unconditional love to feed on to grow healthy. Our children are the ones who have the right to take for themselves all the unconditional love that we can transmit to them as adults, without having anything in return but to make them grow healthy, recognized, and accepted.

Putting conditions in the love that is given to children means telling them that they can be loved only if we need them, only if they will be useful to our ego. Once adults, they will repay our unconditional love with true and healthy love.

The Choice

Let's stay a little longer on another powerful word, the choice: the choice to make available our cleanest and most beautiful energies for ourselves and others with the only purpose of achieving shared pleasure.

The choice for giving love to whoever we want, when we want, or when we can.

When we are codependent, the choice to give love goes through our old triple pact: it stopped being a choice and became a necessity, and an implicit double obligation: "I feel the need to love you, you must feel the need to love me". In the most serious and sometimes pathological cases, the choice becomes obsession, and it seems impossible to stop giving love not only to those who forced us with manipulation, but even to those who asked us to receive less, or not to receive more.

"I have to love you, if I don't, you won't have any reasons to be with me. If I fill you with love, you will not be able to abandon me."

But now the pact has been broken: How many people have left us because they perceived our love as dense and complicated, after all, toxic because it was based not on our choice but the sacrifice of ourselves?

How many times have we felt abandoned and betrayed by people whom we considered ungrateful and who had the only fault of having broken our bond with them?

They weren't always there to manipulate us, sometimes, they only respected our codependency even though they didn't fully understand it and didn't call it by its name. They felt it and simply refused to take it on, in a healthy way, a way that now we can see for what it was and no longer offends us. Out of unconscious pacts, it fills us with gratitude because they did not have the arrogance to want to change us, they simply moved away from us.

If we have broken our triple pact, now we will be able to see it, to hear it, we will hear the words they have told us and we will perceive a different meaning, a different sound, a special warmth.

If you break the pact, I propose that you make another one, I did it and I am infinitely grateful for it: I choose to make available my cleanest and most beautiful energies for myself and others with the sole purpose of achieving shared pleasure.

This is my new and conscious pact for the rest of my life.

Do you believe in these words? They are yours, allow them to enter you, and be part of you. The rest will come by itself; words know for themselves what to do.

No darkness, no fog, no narcissism, no codependency, just clean, conscious, and simple love.

If you trust them, here you have the key for moving the second step through the healing from codependency. Trust them and here you have your new pact for the rest of your life.

Falling in Love

No discussion about love can omit one of the most beautiful, appetizing, exciting, and uplifting moments in life: falling in love.

Is falling in love the most sublime moment of love? Especially if reciprocated, falling in love gives us shared pleasure. Non-shared falling in love makes us suffer (a lot) but remains a precious element of our lives.

So, if we had to make this idea of love on our own, how would we experience falling in love? Is falling in love, love?

When we are falling in love with someone we can't stop thinking about that person, sometimes, we feel frankly obsessed but also very pleasantly obsessed with a person. Should this be considered love?

Should be the person we are falling in love worthy of our love for the simple fact of making us fall in love?

When somebody really makes us vibrate in such an engaging and an overwhelming way, what we feel is passion, curiosity, excitement and sometimes joy.

Sometimes, our feeling is closer to a stomach ache, to be honest (it depends on how much fear we have to be rejected) but in general terms, we can all say that falling in love is something splendidly positive to live and save in our most precious memories.

But even with the wonderfulness of falling in love, it is not necessary to confuse falling in love with love to pay homage to it in its importance.

In such a beautiful condition of falling in love, we are not ready yet to make our love available.

For one reason, we have not chosen to love that person yet. The choice, once again the choice.

Most likely, we will choose it very soon, but not yet, we are not ready because while we are falling in love we still cannot choose.

Even if passion or the obsession of falling in love is so pleasant and beautiful, it is not we the ones who choose, it is our chemistry, it is our body or our soul, but falling in love is not chosen, it just appears.

Let's enjoy every one of those wonderful moments but let's not talk about love yet, because we still don't know if that person who is giving us such beautiful emotions and feelings will be able, or will know, or will want to repay our love using the same coin, love, for us.

If it is so, we will know very soon. If this is not the case, we will have let a beautiful thing like falling in love just be beautiful.

We will have taken it for what it was, avoiding to hand over our precious love in the hands of those who cannot pay for it; in the hands of the incorrect person or worse in the hands of a narcissist, a manipulator, people who are unable to understand the immense value of our wealth, of our coins called love that they do not possess.

The choice to make available our cleanest and most beautiful energies for ourselves and others, with the only purpose of achieving shared pleasure is a choice that comes by itself.

It comes when we understand that our love is great but not infinite, it needs the others' love to regenerate itself, to grow noble and safe.

Sex and Codependency

Sexuality is often a very important connection in a couple, sometimes it's what unites us more than anything else. Other times it is not so essential, but it still determines how happy or comfortable we feel with our partners. Sexuality lays bare our codependent nature. As codependents, we can reach an excellent sexual understanding with our partners. Besides, what better lover than the one who will be so attentive to the pleasures and desires of his or her partner?

If we are codependent, we can't ignore that the chances of making sexuality a source of suffering exist, especially if we experience our sexuality according to the codependent filter of inadequacy.

Sometimes, sexuality recurs in our life as something that somehow escapes our control. When we are codependent it's difficult to say "No", not less important, we can experience sex as a need to please but we don't give the same importance to derive pleasure from it.

The chances of feeling sexually used increase, even in those cases where there is no sexual abuse in legal terms. The possibility of using our sexuality as a basis for starting a relationship increases as well if we are codependents.

A common result can be the need to be sexy and sensual at all costs, or the need to preserve a sexual passion that sooner or later fades in us or our partner. Causing what? Inadequacy.

In the codependent relationship, as well as for love, we feel that our bodies give pleasure but do not receive it. We feel that our whole being is pleasing but does not receive or at least does not receive pleasure in the same measure. This brings us back to the deeper nature of the codependent: giving too much but receiving too little.

I do think it happens to any person who has violated the agreement to give by choice and for shared pleasure. Codependent or not.

Sexuality embraces a huge field, impossible to deal within a single book, it goes from sensual and spiritual love to the most creative pornography, it is not the time to judge, everyone is free to live their sexuality in the way they believe.

It does not matter if we experience our sexuality as atheistic or religious people, if we have sex only to have children, simply to have pleasure or for the pleasure of getting both of them.

Our sexuality changes with stable or occasional partners; rules are different, but the dignity of the people involved is equally important as well as their right to feel good.

If we always apply the same key of interpretation, that of choice and shared pleasure, this would apply to any form of sexuality, but not to run the risk of deviating on such a broad and important topic for human nature, let's focus not on sexuality but only on what we call "making love."

When does "making love" make us feel used?

Sometimes, it's for obvious reasons, we feel forced, abused, we feel we are doing things that we haven't chosen, that we don't like or that we don't like at that precise moment or with that specific person. It is not necessary to be codependent to find ourselves in these situations and, in those cases, it's not difficult to understand the reason for our discomfort, we recognize the abuse which in this case is violent.

The painful consequences are well known and unfortunately, often long psychotherapeutic support will be required.

The not-recognized abuse is the more implicit or less violent from a physical point of view, but especially if is subtle, constant and repetitive over time, it has consequences, like violent abuse.

Sex in exchange for forgiveness, often also for forgiveness that has no reason to be, sex in exchange for a favor, for a concession or attention; sex in exchange for anything other than shared pleasure often introduces the dynamic of invisible abuse.

If we are codependents, the most difficult part to manage is that, despite feeling the discomfort that this causes, we cannot fully understand the reason.

When this happens, our confusion comes from having mixed, without realizing, two worlds that should be very far away, but we have involuntary overlapped. We mixed the rules of "making love" with invisible rules of "abuse".

Every time we find ourselves voluntarily offering or having to give our body for a reason that is not the pure and simple choice of shared pleasure, the annoying sensation of being abused will intervene. Even in those cases not really perceived on a conscious level but perfectly perceived from the bottom of ourselves.

The so called "minimal things" are relevant if they come from our partner, especially if repeated over time until they become normalcy:

"I see you are tired, I do it on behalf of you" but then you can't say no." "I was so kind to you, how can you tell me no?"

He or she is punishing you by a long silence and you would like to come back to a serene life in couple, but you know what you must do.

For sure there is not shared pleasure in this, is there a choice? Maybe. There is not a violent obligation and it can be called choice if we want. Nowadays, I prefer to think that if somebody is kind to me that's because I just deserve kindness.

If somebody is punishing me, I prefer to share my body in another moment. If a receive a favor when I am tired, I will be pleased to offer similar support.

A few years ago, my perception was pretty different, and I fully agreed with them. I couldn't say "no"…

None of these examples in themselves can cause serious harm but they take on serious repetition day after day…until they become our normal sexuality.

Especially because once we accept this dynamic with a partner as subtly imposed or fomented in a more or less voluntary way, we activate a type of relationship that will hardly disappear on its own and more likely could escape of our hands if we have a codependent tendency.

It would be a pure illusion to pretend to be able to heal from codependency if we do not dwell on the enormous importance that sexuality can have in our lives.

It doesn't matter if we experience it as Christians, Atheists, teenagers or as elders.

Sexuality is always sexuality. "Making love" means "making love" regardless of who makes it with us, when we make it, and how many times.

Each time it has the same dignity, each time it is worth in itself, each time it will have the importance that we and the other person would have chosen to give it. Each time we should know which pact we are loyal to, and what meaning we have given to love if we want to make love by feeling that we choose to do it in shared pleasure.

What About Seduction?

In seduction, it's quite normal to offer favors, gifts, special attention, coins that do not pay for love. The goal of seduction can be love, other times, definitely not. Should we, therefore, give up seducing and be seduced? Can be seduction a beautiful part of love? As far as I am concerned, yes It can.

But we also have to say that seduction it's a quite sensitive topic in codependency. It can activate unpleasant feelings or even unpleasant consequences when we are codependents.

If we want to seduce somebody, our seduction can be contaminated by our tendency to "give too much". It does not sound so strange, if we are codependents, we have this tendency.

The thing is that in seduction we are placing the basis of a relationship with the person we want to stay with, regardless if it's for a short period of time or forever. Depending on this basis, we will be deciding how to connect with another person in the next hours, days, months, or even years.

Giving too much in seduction means, for example, to be too sexy and sensual. Who can decide if we are just sexy and sensual or "too" sexy and "too" sensual? The correct answer should be nobody can, but within toxic sentimental relationships this answer would not be the correct one.

Codependent

The sensuality we show will be manipulated later, and suddenly, we find ourselves in the position to pay the price of non-existent bills.

For example, as codependents we face two common situations:

a) Implicitly, we become "sexual pleasure suppliers". So, we have to give pleasure, but we are not supposed to receive it.

b) Implicitly or explicitly, our relations seem based only on sensuality, so sexual attraction comes to be the only common language to be together. Once again, it is not right or wrong itself, but it's an expensive approach with no exit clause.

Basically, the hidden manipulative message of this is: Weren't you sexy and sensual? Well, from now on you can't stop being sexy and sensual.

Up to now, we are leaving aside the unhealthy concept of seduction as the conquest of a body, a concept that recalls war concepts.

It opens a broad ethical and cultural discourse that would be out of topic here. But this is the only concept of seduction we can find in the mind of narcissists, psychopaths, and other types of manipulators.

Sometimes, in our life as codependents, they are the only seducers we have been in touch with, and the risk to perceive the seduction only as a dirty and hateful practice is sadly frequent.

With them, it's not relevant at all if we are seducing or being seduced, the result is unhealthy and toxic anyway, and it converts us in the victim of manipulation.

Seduction is in itself fun, pleasant, and a caress for our self-esteem.

If sincere, seduction is a fantastic bomb of excitement and pleasure. Indeed, blessed be it, it is a reach taste for our life.

One of the most romantic phrases that I had the pleasure of hearing was that of a 67-year-old husband who commenting on a sad story that occurred in his country, in front of cameras said: "I am 67 years old, I met my wife when I was 18, we got married 45 years ago, and we still feel the pleasure of seducing each other!" My standing ovation for them.

Out of narcissistic "love bombing", out of toxic or violent relationships, seduction has safe rules, it's just a way to create a connection between two unknown people and it's an excellent aperitif for love.

Even if we accept that, it would be important to accept also that seduction has its own coin and it's not love.

If we exchange it for the love coin, we will feel used sooner or later, deceived, alone, or betrayed.

If we choose to exchange seduction with seduction, we will let ourselves play a safe game.

We will give what another one is ready to give us, with the shared pleasure of enjoying each other, in seduction. Not in love yet, just in seduction.

This closes the doors to manipulators but if seduction let us meet the right person to stay with, we will have another nice photo for the album of our good memories and, if love will be, much better for everyone, many other photos and a good story will follow together.

Having said that, as codependents, we are all fully aware that seduction touches our more intimate fibers and it is important to give dignity to our choice to do not feel comfortable in it.

When it happens, it means it is not shared pleasure and it is fine.

Codependent

CONCLUSION

I do hope it was a shared pleasure and I hope everything that allowed me to understand my old pacts with myself and with others will be useful for you and your loved ones.

In this book, we have seen scientific evidence and personal vicissitudes.

Limits are the size of every grandness, but it means that in love we are more alone and also freer to decide what is love for us.

If as said, our healing from codependency only can pass through our love, depending on the meaning of love we chose, a long list of things will change in our lives and quite quickly.

Love is loyalty and it's important to be fully aware of where we are putting our loyalty and why. Love is a contribution. Every one of us should be able to change in the name of safe and simple love, it contributes to improving many people's lives.

Take care of yourself.

Love,

Michelle J. West

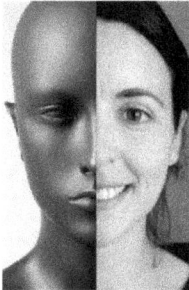

Codependent

CPSIA information can be obtained
at www.ICGtesting.com
Printed in the USA
BVHW041516230621
610126BV00015B/3076

9 781803 253800